COLOR TESTING

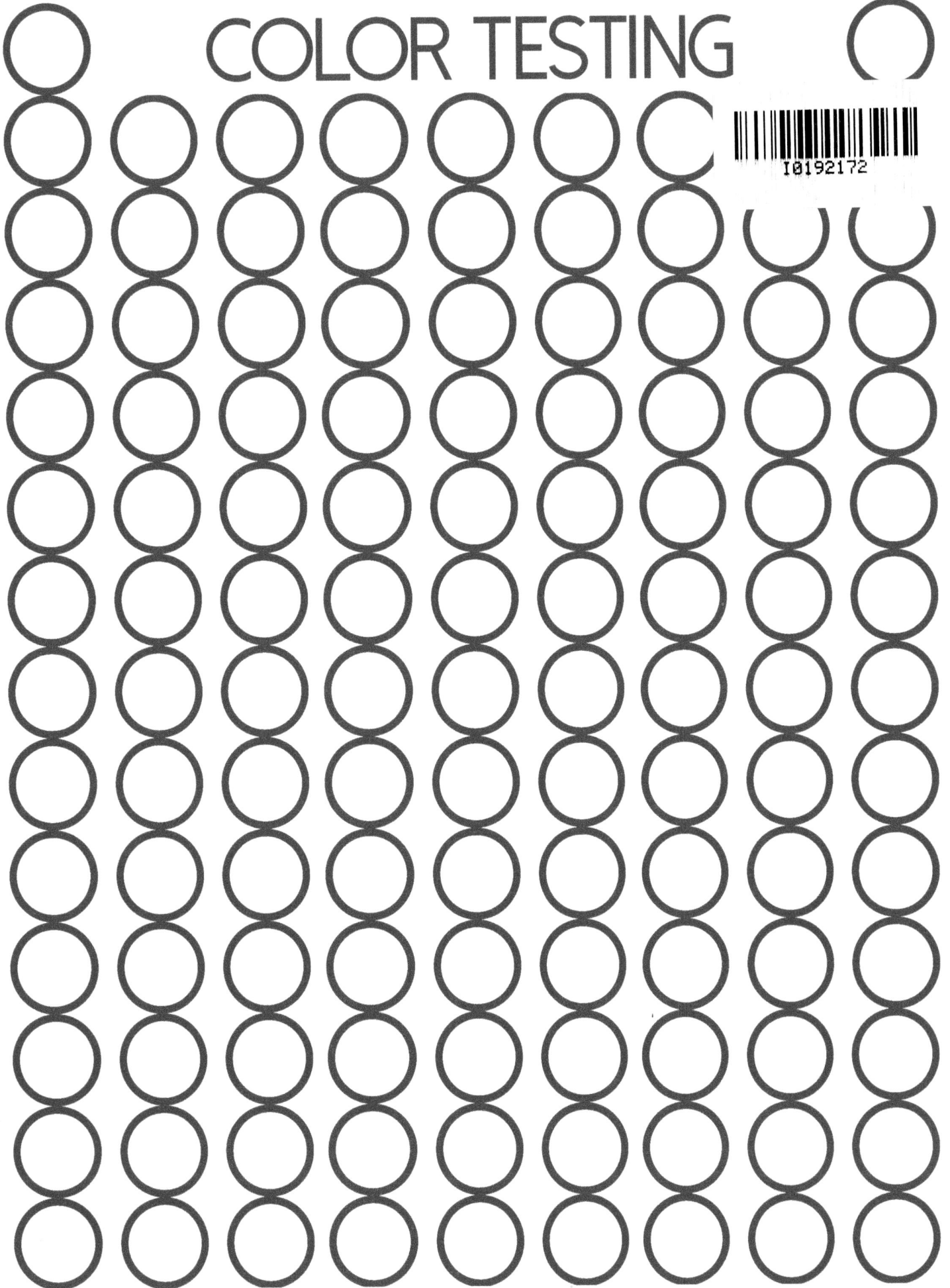

Happy Holly*Day

Christmas can't be bought from a store...
Maybe Christmas means a little bit more. ~ Dr. Suess

An adult coloring book filled with 41 Christmas themed designs.

Give yourself a break from the hustle and bustle of the holiday season and enjoy some good old fashioned coloring book fun and relaxation with the whimsical & unique designs by Dawné Dominique and D. Thomas Jerlo.

PLEASE NOTE: This is not a children's coloring book.
Images are intricately detailed and will require 100% of your attention.

ENJOY!

Copyright © 2017 Dawné Dominique
ISBN: 978-1-7750442-6-0
Cover and Art Designed by Dawné Dominique
Vector Copyrights © VectorStock & DepositPhotos

Published by DusktilDawn Publications
www.dusktildawndesigns.com
CANADA

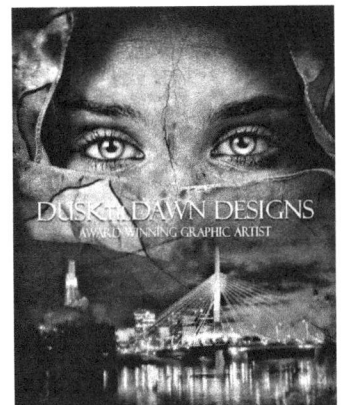

COLOR TESTING

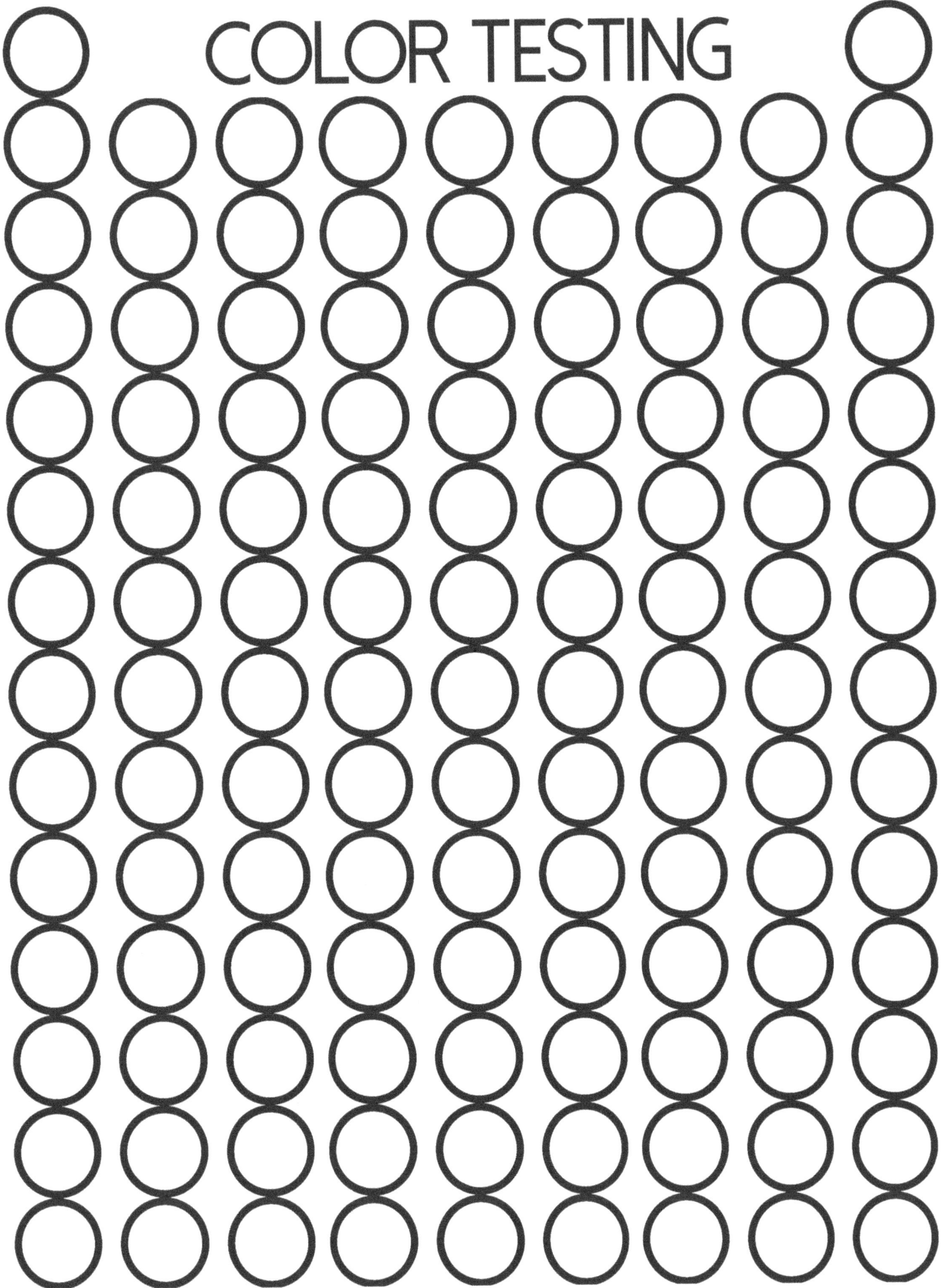

IF YOU ENJOYED THIS COLORING BOOK, DON'T BE SHY...LEAVE A REVIEW.

Check out other adult coloring books by Dawné Dominique & D. Thomas-Jerlo

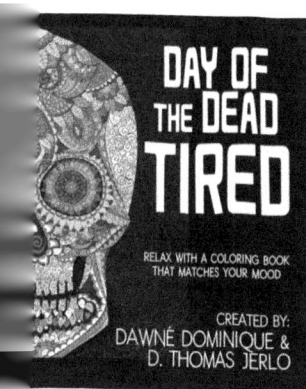

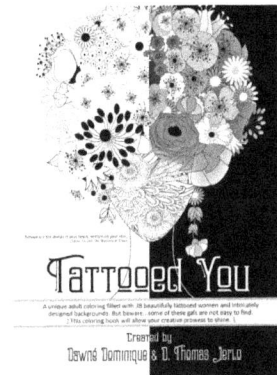

www.lulu.com/spotlight/dusktildawn

Also available at:

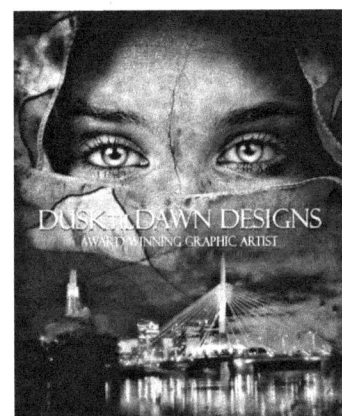

DUSKTILDAWN DESIGNS
AWARD-WINNING GRAPHIC ARTIST

www.dusktildawndesigns.com